I AM A BABY BOOMER

MADE IN THE U.S.A.

Once upon a time there was
a Baby Boomer,
Made in the U.S.A.

I am

LYNN GREEN

And she lived happily ever after

BALBOA.
PRESS
A DIVISION OF HAY HOUSE

Balboa Press books may be ordered through booksellers or by contacting:

Balboa Press
A Division of Hay House
1663 Liberty Drive
Bloomington, IN 47403
www.balboapress.com
1 (877) 407-4847

Because of the dynamic nature of the Internet, any web addresses or links contained
in this book may have changed since publication and may no longer be valid. The views
expressed in this work are solely those of the author and do not necessarily reflect the
views of the publisher, and the publisher hereby disclaims any responsibility for them.

The author of this book does not dispense medical advice or prescribe the use
of any technique as a form of treatment for physical, emotional, or medical
problems without the advice of a physician, either directly or indirectly. The
intent of the author is only to offer information of a general nature to help you
in your quest for emotional and spiritual well-being. In the event you use any
of the information in this book for yourself, which is your constitutional right,
the author and the publisher assume no responsibility for your actions.

Any people depicted in stock imagery provided by Thinkstock are models,
and such images are being used for illustrative purposes only.
Certain stock imagery © Thinkstock.

Print information available on the last page.

ISBN: 978-1-5043-7965-6 (sc)
ISBN: 978-1-5043-7967-0 (hc)
ISBN: 978-1-5043-7966-3 (e)

Library of Congress Control Number: 2017906643

Balboa Press rev. date: 05/01/217

DEDICATION

To my Mom and Dad with Love,

I picked the best!!!

ACKNOWLEDGEMENTS

To my sister Karin --

I am grateful for your positive message to keep writing.
Karin told me--"This is the beginning
of something extraordinary!"

CHAPTER

1

I will start in 1966. It is a glorious time to be a ten year old. I am Lynn, born in Bloomington Indiana and am the oldest of three children. I have a sister, a brother and my mom and dad are the best. We, "the baby boomers" are literally everywhere. In other words, there are a lot of kids in our neighborhood, approximately 100 children per street. Our family lives in a suburb of Detroit in Madison Heights Michigan.

We moved here from Indiana. Dad is from Ohio originally, moved to Indiana and met my mother in grade school. Mom is an only child and one of those super intelligent women that had straight A's on every single report card. We were reminded regularly as report card time approached. Dad is an engineer genius who always looked so sharp when dressed in his suits for work. He always had the real-deal handkerchief in his pocket and wore fancy shoes that required a shoe tree at the end of each day. After Dad graduated from Indiana University, we moved to Kokomo Indiana where my sister Karin was born. Dad's company moved us to Michigan in 1958 where my brother Jeff was born. This was where the car industry was happening and the best place for a job for dad.

Turning ten years old is a big deal, so as the month of March gets here, I ask my mother if I can pick out a new pair of shoes for a birthday gift. I am in love with PF flyers. In my opinion they are the coolest tennis shoes on earth. At the shoe store the salesman greets us and asks, "what are you looking for?" We have a seat and I tell him. He quickly brings a foot measuring devise over and I stand on it to get my shoe size. He then brings my new shoes from a back-room, and slides over in front of me on his stool. He places a shoe on the incline part of the stool and I try it on. Feels good! I put the other shoe on and he ties both shoes, very tight! Why does the shoe salesman always tie my shoes too tight? He slaps the side of one shoe and says walk around in them. Now for the test run. Mom always has me walk over to her so she may push on the toe part of the shoe to make sure it's a good fit. She also asks me if the arch is good enough. We always check out the arch of a new shoe! I'm sure, this is so I can run faster and jump higher. My shoes also come with a groovy decoder ring.

I also get to invite a few girl friends over for cake and ice-cream and then go to a movie. After we eat our chocolate cake and I open some gifts, it's time to get our coats and boots on and load up in the car. We get to the movie theatre and all jump out of the car and trudge through about six inches of slush and snow to get to the theatre door. Inside, we get our box of popcorn and find our seats in the theatre. The movie I picked is The Ghost and Mr. Chicken. This turned out to be a scary movie. It's funny to watch your friends stare at the movie screen with huge open eyes and chew popcorn really fast.

I often wonder how my parents did such a great job of "doing life".

They are so good at it, like professionals. Everything is humming along nicely, Dad, Mom, three kids and a dog. One thing that does not thrill me, is mom serving lima beans at dinner time. We are told to eat what's on our plates--there are four food groups, don't ya know! Mom used to make cheese sauce to put over the broccoli, but nothing could save these little dry paste-like lima things. It was interesting in those days; we ate our vegetables because our mother said we had too; our parents had goofy rules all the time.

Saturday, in my mind was definitely designed for relaxing and watching cartoons and Sir Graves Ghastly, but mom had a Saturday rule. This was the day that all beds must be stripped and all sheets, pillowcases and blankets were to be washed and the house had to be dusted and vacuumed from top to bottom. To say that I dislike dusting is a huge understatement. It's because of mom's large nick-nack collection, her fancy tea cups in particular. This dislike carries over into my adult life which manifested into a no nick-nack policy. Funny, that makes me want to sing "nick-nack patty-wack, give a dog a bone. This old man came rolling home."

So back to dusting, I figured out how to make it into a fun game. The cups and saucers would be lined up for the dusting spray attack. I would aim as best as possible to get it done very quickly. I usually ended up using a lot more spray than necessary, but efficiency to get the job done quickly was top priority. I had to get back to my cartoons after all. Dad put into effect the TV watching rule, we had to sit at least six feet from the television which I thought was totally unnecessary. It's funny how nobody ever measured the six feet or got a straight answer as to why he made such a silly rule at all. Anyway, my sister, brother and I would sneak the yucky lima beans to our dog Angus, which I believe made him the most healthy dog on the block. Our dinner prayer went like this: "God is Great, God is good, Let us thank him for our food. Angus thanks you too. Amen."

I think I will give my grandparents credit for the great job they did raising my parents. They were strict back then, and you did mind your manners! Everyone was polite and respectful towards one another, especially your elders. My Great grandmother Lottie was so awesome. She was born in 1895 and basically raised my mother. Lottie's daughter, my grandmother Grace, was a working woman as her husband passed away. Both Grandmas lived together in Indiana. Great grandma is a wonderful person and it seems she always has my back. Once in a while I would find myself in some mischief or, I put too much Hershey's syrup on my ice cream; my mother would discipline me. Great grandma would say, "Leave her be, Jannie". And add "God love her." She was the best!

When Great grandma would come for a week long visit, we would all load up in the car and drive to the Detroit train station. Great grandma would always travel by train, she never did learn how to drive a car and mentioned to us that she never rode a bike or roller skated either. I always wondered why she didn't bike ride or roller skate, now I wish I would have asked her why. The train station was like a whole different world. So much noise and activity and the trains are huge! As we walked down the long walkway to greet Great grandma, the excitement grew. It was a bit of a walk in between two giant trains. Such an awesome experience, just walking and watching everyone else greeting a loved one or observing the luggage being stacked on large carts to be rolled into the station. I remember holding either my mother or father's hand tightly, it was a large, loud, scary place. The trains made loud hissing sounds and people were noisy as they spoke. We would wait patiently for Great grandma to come to the train door and walk down the stairs and step stool. We ran up to her and gave her big hugs and watched mom and dad as they also hugged and kissed her. After gathering the luggage, Great grandma would always buy my sister, brother and me a comic book. We would go into a little store in the train station and each of us would try to choose the perfect one. I remember "Casper the Friendly Ghost" was one of my favorite. She also bought my sister, brother and me a Tootsie Roll. The comic books were only twelve cents each, and the Tootsie Rolls were large and only a few cents as well.

On the way home from the train station, Great grandma sat in the front seat of our car while dad drove. We liked when mom sat in the back seat with us. Dad pulled into a gas station and up to the gas pump, where a young man was standing. Dad rolled down his window and said, "fill-er-up please." As we all sat in the car, the attendant filled up our car with gas and cleaned off the front window. My Great grandma decided to help the attendant and point, and then tap her finger on the window where he missed a spot. He quickly moved his squeegee over the spot and smiled and waved to us all. We were all giggling in the back seat; I thought Great grandma was brave and funny.

On the way home, we all start looking through our new comic books. It's funny, my mother doesn't like when I remind her how she made us clean out our comic book collections when we were young and place them in the trash. I argued with her to keep them, not knowing they would be worth big bucks someday--man-oh-man, we had a lot of comic books!

My grandmothers were such nice people. Lottie's daughter, Grace, as a working woman, decided to purchase a small cottage on a lake in Indiana. We had summers loaded with so much fun! She had a pontoon boat that was great to ride around on in the evenings. She would putter us around the edge of the lake, close enough to wave to the neighbors. During the day, the speed boat was in full use. My grandmother was an excellent water skier. She would use just one ski and turn all the way around in a circle while we watched in amazement. We would clap and sing praises. She tried to teach all of us how to ski, but I decided along with my sister and brother to just stick to swimming around the lake. Skiing was a difficult balancing act we could not get the hang of. The lake had several channels we would go swimming up and down. Now I understand why mom put us all in swimming lessons for so many years when we were young. We would disappear for several hours just swimming down channel after channel. I liked to pretend to be a spy and watch the people at the other cottages. I would swim slowly and as quiet as possible past them, with only my eyes peeking out of the water. The channels were connected to each other through very large silver drainage pipes which we would swim through without a second thought. The insect life was quite active in there, have you ever seen water spiders? They just walk on the water, and when you get near them they shoot across the top of the water so fast. Pretty cool really.

We also learned how to fish. I am among many that are not happy to touch a worm, they are so gross! I decided to be the supervisor/observer of the fishing expeditions. I was then happily free from worm touching. The one time I did decide to fish, my grandmother's boyfriend, Ed, said he would put a worm on the hook for me. I liked Ed, he was always a snappy dresser and was very nice to me. So he put a worm on my hook, and I threw the line into the water. As soon as I did, I caught my first fish. It was a pretty good size catfish! Ed said I should try not to catch a catfish because they are difficult to remove from the hook. I thought to myself, maybe he should have told the worm not to get eaten by a catfish-sheesh, silly grown-ups. Fishing turned out to be fun, I always enjoyed being out on the boat with my family.

In the evening when we were done playing and it was time to set up the lawn chairs and get the barbeque started for dinner, the mosquitos were really terrible. Not to worry, grandma had a fogger machine. My grandma is "super grandma", I like how she is prepared for everything. She filled this large, gas-powered blower machine with some bug killer and started it up. It looks like a leaf blower with a short snout. She would start walking across her yard making sure she was aiming down wind. As the fog was shooting out of the blower, it looked like a big white cloud hovering on her lawn. As the gentle breeze moved the fog across her whole yard, it took out the mosquitos! I wonder what the heck that chemical was.

My father's mother was our church goer. Willadine was a Seventh day Adventist. We would go to church on Saturday with her when we visited in Indiana. There was a kid's class of course; and it seemed to be a nice place. I remember they had several different donation baskets, and my grandmother gave us each one nickel. I never knew which basket was the correct one; I guess God didn't really mind.

When church was over, we would go back to Grandma and Grandpa's house for a nice big family dinner. I remember how wonderful it smelled with dinner cooking, and there was always the slight hint of Bengay in the air too. Grandma and Grandpa always had two Chihuahuas and two Lazy- Boy chairs that I always loved to sit in with the doggies. They would hop up on my lap for a good belly-rub.

Grandma Willadine was a bit strict, not in a mean way, just old fashioned standards. Good old manners and common courtesy; good stuff.

I remember telling her I had a grilled cheese with mustard on it for breakfast one morning. She said to me, "I never heard tell such a thing."

CHAPTER

Back in Michigan

In our little house we had three bedrooms, so my sister and I had to share one. We were opposite-type gals; she was a girly-girl, cheerleader and I was the drummer-girl / tom boy. On my birthday or at Christmas time, I always gave the Barbie dolls to my sister immediately after receiving them. I still don't get the point! Have you ever stepped on a Barbie doll high-heel shoe in your bare feet? There's something you don't forget. All I really wanted as a gift, instead of a doll, was a Varoom motor for my bike. I never did get one, so I used a clothespin to attach playing cards to my bike. I thought I was so clever when I doubled up the cards to hit my bike spokes for even more noise. As soon as I was sure all cards were tightly fastened to my bike, I would test drive down the street adding in a few wheelies for fun. Such a good feeling of accomplishment; everything stayed on my bike, including me.

It was interesting how Karin and I had a definite line-down-the-middle of our bedroom. My sister was very messy, and my side of the room was so fabulous!

Pictures of Bedroom

Before bedtime each night, my sister, brother and I would get our baths and then brush our teeth. Some evenings we may have to initiate "Bubble gum, Bubble gum, in a dish, how many Bubble gum do you wish" or someone would count, 1, 2, 3, and we would yell "not it!". Nobody wanted to go first.

We each had our own designated colored Dixie cup. My parents shared the yellow cup, I had the red one, Karin green, and Jeff blue. The cups all stacked up neatly in the cup holder on the wall with all of our toothbrushes hanging around the outside in their own little hanger slot. Not too sanitary really, but we all survived. I'm glad we are a hand washing family.

My brother's room was next door to ours. In the evenings when we were in bed and supposed to be sleeping, my brother would knock on the wall. Karin's bed was next to the wall so she would knock back. We decided to make up code words for the number of knocks on the wall. Three knocks was, "how are you?", two knocks was "fine", and one knock was "shut up". Sometimes we would almost be asleep and Jeff would knock on the wall. He received a loud, one knock in response. Other times Karin would start the wall conversation and our mother would end it. She would yell upstairs to us. "Stop making that noise, and go to sleep!" Yikes! And that was it, all done.

As the work week begins, dad is off to work while mom makes sure we are all up and preparing for the school day. We walk to school each day (uphill both ways), so we look out the front window to see what the weather looks like outside. Do we need boots? Rain coats? Mittens? I remember when it was just raining, not snowing, we could wear our rubbers instead of boots. Now that was an excellent invention, I thought. Just slip this little rubber shoe cover over your shoes and wa-la! Good to go. We didn't need to wear our bulky boots. When we got into school each day we would all hang up our coats, change into shoes, and line up our boots or rubbers and then get to our desks. Before the school day could actually start, we would all stand up, put our right hands over our hearts and say the Pledge of Allegiance to the Flag. We were very proud to be Americans. After that, homework assignments were turned in and the learning lessons began. I remember one day, we were supposed to write 500 times, "I will not talk in class" for homework. This was because one of the bad boys would not be quiet the day before. I had much better things to do, so I did not write the sentences. Why should I? When the teacher noticed I did not turn in the sentences, she called me up to the front of the classroom, to her desk and asked me why I did not do the assignment. I told her I was not talking in class so I didn't feel it was a fair assignment. She told me to go back to my desk and sit down, so I walked quickly back to my desk. Phew, I was a bit scared.

Each day we would walk home for lunch. (uphill) Most moms were home back in the day, and my mom could really make a mean pot of chicken noodle soup. Add a few soda crackers and that was a delicious meal. So why did we call them soda crackers? Answer: They are made from flour, yeast and… wait for it…baking soda! Ta da! That can be our, something new learned for the day. I try to acknowledge something new I've learned every day. Ok, so when we were done eating, it was back to school. We settle in for an afternoon of reading, writing, and arithmetic.

I really did enjoy school; we actually had teachers that took time to teach us. They encouraged us to ask questions, and always said there are never any stupid questions.

When school time ends, the safety patrol heads out to their posts. We had a huge safety patrol. Every street corner in the neighborhood was covered. We all feel safe and everyone seems happy to be living in our "Leave it to Beaver"- type neighborhood.

My sister and I attended dance class once a week after school. Tap, ballet, acrobatics and jazz at Borgo Sisters school of Dance. Mom would pull up to our elementary school, to pick us up. We would jump in our 1964 Pontiac Catalina, powder blue of course, and off we would go. That was my favorite car! It was in the popular class we called "the boat cars". They were very big, and ours had a big engine; it was very fast. I remember the day our family went to the dealership to buy our car. Mom got behind the wheel to take us for a test drive. As we pulled up to a stop sign to exit the parking lot, mom began to brake, and we were all jerked to a stop. Mom screamed," I can't drive this car, it has power brakes!" We all just sat very quietly until dad spoke up and said, "you pretty much have to, all the new cars have power brakes now."

Mom always did the speed limit even though we were in a huge rush to get to dance on time. Our dance clothes were waiting, ready for us to quickly change into. Karin and I were very good at changing into our tights and leotards in the spacious back seat. We always were dressed by the time we got to class, mom gets credit for our efficient dressing routine. Mom would give us a quick shout, "quit fooling around back there and get dressed!" We turned out to be pretty good little dancers too. One year a select group of us were honored to perform a Can-Can dance at the Royal Oak Lions Club Show.

Lynn and Karin

During the summer months I would ride my bike alone with a radio hanging from my handle bars. It's on the station CKLW of course, and I'm listening to the popular songs play; yes, some are The Beatles. It's such a beautiful day; I will peddle by a few girlfriends houses to see if anybody wants to do something. I pull up to Mary's house and call her. "Mary!, Mary!" I sing at the door. She comes out and we begin to cruise the streets.

We listen very carefully for any garage band that may be practicing. Bands are popping up all through the neighborhood. One of my favorites was "3 + 1." The drummer was a girl! That's when I knew I would be a percussionist.

We decide to ride our bikes over to Suicide Hill, this is so much fun! There's nothing like flying down a mountain-type hill at 142 miles per hour, on a little sting ray bike! Soon to be discovered, it doesn't have the best brakes. Sooo much fun!! We didn't really scream; we just held on so darn tight to those handle bars and flew like the wind, what a rush! I do remember being grateful for a safe landing and thinking the next trip down, I will apply my brakes beginning at the top of the mountain.

Back on the road again, we see Mr. Wren, our milkman, doing his route. He stops his delivery truck and jumps out with some milk. Running up to a house, he opens the milk chute and places the milk in. Before he gets back to his delivery truck, we beg him for some of his crushed ice. After splashing us in the face with the melted, dripping water, he hands us a glob of crushed ice; it's so delicious! We thank him, and he continues on his way, and so do we.

As we make it to the other end of our subdivision, we swing by the 5 & 10 drugstore. Mary and I each have a few quarters and decide to buy a candy treat, I load up on Pez, and I end up eating half of it before I get it into my dispenser. It takes too long, and I can't wait.

We decide to see about some lunch and grab a quick sandwich at my house. Next we go by Debbie's house and call her. We sing… "Debbie!, Debbie!." She comes out. On to Linda's house, "Linda!, Linda!" we sing. Out she comes, and we all ride off. After we ride around for a little while we decide to relax a bit and get a blanket and a deck of cards. It's so nice to sit under a tree and play a game of cards or get the Parcheesi game going.

As we sit on the blanket playing our card game I hear a loud bing…..bong…..bing…..bong. It's the popular knife-sharpening guy! You never know when he will show up riding his big three-wheeler bike with his sharpening equipment on board. All of the sudden people start running out of their houses towards him as he pulls over to the curb. You can hear a mother yelling, "stop running with knives!" That's a good rule. Isn't it great when you see someone who thinks of an idea like door-to-door knife sharpening, and it's a success? This was such a great convenience for us, and the knife guy started a business that most likely paid his bills with a good income.

We all decided to go into my backyard and get the Jarts game out and play a bit. This was an incredibly fun game made up of four large darts-- two blue and two red ones, each about a foot long. Each Jart had a weighted metal tip on one end and three plastic fins on a rod at the other end. You throw them underhand toward the horizontal ground target. The target was a plastic ring, and if you're Jart landed in the yellow plastic circle, you would get a point. All is going well, and my girlfriends and I are having fun throwing these missiles from one end of my yard to the other. I'm not sure who tried to throw it overhand first, but this was an interesting development. Man, these things can really fly when you whip them overhand. It's interesting that we never read the box that our Jarts game came in. It says "An outdoor game for adults" There was also a Warning: Not a toy for use by children. May cause serious or fatal injury. Read instructions carefully. Keep out of reach of children. Oops!! I never really knew there were directions. We never had any issues with anyone getting hurt with this game, but in the 1980's, I understand that many careless people did cause injuries. In December of 1988 the sale of lawn darts was banned in the United States. It makes me wonder how so many baby boomers played this game in the late 1960's and early 1970's, without it having to be banned.

As the days become warmer, family pools start opening up. Mary's dad bought an awesome above-ground pool. Big enough for quite a lot of us.

We all ride our bikes over with bathing suits on, towels draped around our shoulders and our licker-lockers on. For some reason our family called flip flops, licker-lockers; there were two stories why. One was, we thought that's the noise they made when we walked in them, and the second reason I recall was someone couldn't pronounce flip flop, so it became licker-locker. I know, things that make you go hmmmm.

As we all rush to jump in Mary's pool, we start to make a whirlpool. We get it going so fast, then try to go against the current. Nobody drowns, but we do swallow a bit of water. I am grateful for Mary's mom's sign. She posted... "I don't swim in your toilet, so don't pee in my pool!" I thought that was clever. Another activity was to take the inner tube to the middle of the pool and start pushing the water down. As several of us were pushing together, all of the sudden the water was pushing back and we were flying into the air as high as the garage roof, this was a blast! Not for long though. Mary's dad said the pressure of the water is going to push the pool walls out and down. So, no more "flying to the sky' for now. We usually spent the whole day there, with the exception of mealtime breaks. I remember living in my bathing suit all day. When dinner time rolled around, mom would step out onto our front porch and shout out our names. This meant, time for us to come home. Mom put a dry towel on our dinner chair so we would not destroy it; we were soaking wet. She knew as soon as we gobbled down our dinner, we would be right back out the door and down the street back in the pool.

On occasion mom would call us home a little early, and the towel was on the couch. The Awrey bakery man was here. We would sit on the couch while Lyn, our delivery man, would open his two-shelf display of the most delicious looking cakes and coffee cakes you could ever imagine. We all helped decide which luscious treat we were going to purchase. The double-layer chocolate cake was always my favorite. What a beautiful sight.

We did a lot of singing-type yelling in those days. Not just the kids, but parents too. The only time we didn't hear the parents shouting out names to call us in at the end of the day, was when they gave us permission to stay out until the street lights came on.

One fine summer day I found two baby crows and decided to become their mama. After clearing it with my parents, my rescue mission began. I thought they could stay in a box in my bedroom, but mom and dad said that was not acceptable, and I could keep them in their box, in the garage. I agreed and it was a very good thing because crows grow to become very big birds. They are also loud when they decide to start saying "caw, caw". Not to mention, they are not potty trained. I had a large box in the garage with blankets and water. My mother helped in the crow food department. When she went to the Kowalski deli for our weekly meat supply, she bought a hunk of fresh hamburger. The freshly ground beef looked very much like worms. As I dangled the meat over Blacky's and Crow's beaks, they would open their mouths so wide and gobble up the meat very quickly. They made a noise while eating, like yum, yum, yum. It was so cool to see how they would eat, and it was very rewarding to see these little guys survive.

As they began to get bigger, I thought I should teach them to fly. I got our push-broom from the garage. I laid it on the lawn and put Blacky on the handle first; crow would have the second lesson. I took hold of the broom end and slowly moved the handle up and down. It was interesting, when I moved the handle down, they would open their wings and balance.

So Cool!!! After a while they were flapping those wings vigorously, as I moved the broom handle higher and a bit more quick. Some days my arms got so tired from moving the broom up and down with crows on it, they seemed to really like the broom handle ride. It was so cute, I sat the broom down on the ground and they would jump on it, they were very intelligent. The ultimate test was when I decided to put them on my little stingray bike handlebars, one at a time. I rode my bike down the street, with a crow on my bike; they were so darn cool! I loved those crows so much, but I knew they were going to fly away someday soon.

One day we were out and about in the backyard, and Blacky

decided to fly. She flew out into the front yard and up into our tree. I told her, great job-- now come on down and let's get in the garage, it was starting to rain. Well, she looked at me, and I kept looking up at her. She would tilt her head to look down at me as I asked her again and again to come down until I was soaking wet and getting cold. I decided to start walking up the driveway to get in the garage; and when I was almost there, I heard a little "caw". I turned around to see Blacky waddling up the driveway towards me. I ran towards her, scooped her up, gave her a hug, and we went to dry ourselves off in the garage. I just figured she got way up there and was a bit afraid of getting herself down.

Well, they did grow up and started flying around. At first they stayed close by, flying onto our house roof and the neighbor's roofs. One day I put a quarter on the ground to see if it is true, that crows collect shiny objects. All of the sudden Crow swooped down and grabbed the quarter and put it up on the roof. After that happened, I thought I should have used a different object, not my quarter; there goes my Pez cash.

They started flying farther and farther away, and one day they were gone. Today, when I hear a crow or see one, I say hello, and ask if they have a message. The crow is such a beautiful magical bird, and I feel blessed to have had the opportunity to have two as part of my family.

CROW AND ANGUS

DAD / PETE WITH CROW AND BLACKY

On a weekend day, dad introduced a very cool activity to us. He bought a kit to make a rocket that was designed to shoot into the air and then float down after its parachute opened. So after a day of an assembly process, that included an hour of painting, and then a paint-drying period, we were off to our elementary school with our fluorescent pink rocket to see if it works. Dad put the rocket and launch pad in the car to take to the school field, while quite a few friends and I hopped on our bikes and rode to the field. Yay, launch time is here, and we are all doing a countdown. 10, 9, 8, 7, 6, Dad has the fuse lit and it's all systems are go. 5, 4, 3, 2, 1. All of a sudden, that rocket took off with a huge whoosh! We all start yelling, "oh my gosh, look at it go", and "cool!" We are all looking up at the sky, watching it go higher and higher and higher. I am wondering if it's going to keep going and if dad remembered to assemble the parachute part. It stopped climbing, and sure enough he remembered--the parachute popped out, and it started floating down. A couple of things we didn't figure on were how high it was going to go and how far it was going to drift when the wind took it as soon as the parachute opened. We all hopped on our bikes and were off speeding through the neighborhood streets in search of our fluorescent pink rocket. At first I thought a pink rocket was odd; but when you start chasing one, you figure out why it's pink. Green would have been really stupid.

Once we found it, we took it back to the school field and prepared for another launch. Once again, countdown and whoosh, up she went. This thing went so darn high, it was amazing. When the parachute opened this time we were all on our bikes ready to roll. It was incredible that we found it so many times. What fun we had riding all around the neighborhood looking for our rocket.

Its Saturday, dinner time, mom and dad tell us we are going to the Galaxy drive-in after we eat. This was a great idea! Karin, Jeff and I finish eating and run to our bedrooms and put our pajamas on. Mom starts making popcorn and grape Kool-Aid. Dad had purchased a large piece of plywood to place in the backseat of our car. Excellent measuring job! This turns our back-seat area into a huge blanket and pillow comfy spot.

We get there early, so we can go to the playground. After we get our parking spot and pull the speaker in through the car window, we jump out of the car and run through the many rows of parked cars trying to get to the swings before all the other kids. After sliding and swinging for a bit, it gets close to movie time, so we walk over to the concession building and use the restrooms before the movie. When our movie is over, I am sleepy and all it takes is the intermission hotdog, jumping into the bun to put me out. The intermission show is just awful! It's funny how 1800 cars are watching this boring thing.

A different weekend activity was spent at the shooting range. This particular day dad was taking us with him to shoot skeet. Dad had an awesome shotgun that was very loud, so ear plugs were always used. The kids' mission was to retrieve the clay pigeons at a designated time, to be announced by the skeet shooters. A clay pigeon is a round clay disc approximately four and a half inches in diameter. The men who were shooting would take turns yelling "pull", and the pigeon would be launched into the air for them to shoot. Shhhh, don't tell anyone, but sometimes dad's would miss. When the men agreed to a ceasefire, all the kids ran around the huge field looking for the pigeons that were still intact or just slightly hit. When we thought we had them all, we would run back and proudly hand them to our father.

After all the ammunition was spent, we would pack it up and head for home. Dad would save the shells or casings after he shot them and clean them up for the reloading process. He did quite a bit of reloading bullet shells to save money on this hobby. This was so awesome to watch and participate in. The small machines he had with levers and places for weighing different bullet guts were impressive.

After everything was put away for the day, dad would have one more fun thing to do. He made a trail of gunpowder in our driveway in the backyard that went all the way across it. At the end of the trail was an empty soup can, so when dad lit the gunpowder at our end, it started burning super bright--it lit up the whole driveway. The bright, burning gunpowder traveled all the way to the can until it sent that can flying into the air with an amazing explosion. Yay! Now that was cool!

Rainy days, we are trapped in the house, so out comes the Creepy Crawler set, the creation of icky bugs is about to begin.

The goop was carefully poured from the bottle into the molds. Then we would place the mold in the "Thing Maker". The "Thing Maker" is a little stove-type-thing that you set the metal mold in once it's fully heated.

Plug is necessary. When the goop is done cooking, we remove the mold from the heat and set it in the cooling water tray. That was very fun to do, a large cloud of steam rolled up and into the room. After cooled, we remove the rubber bug. Oooooh, creepy. We made many many creepy bugs in all different colors and sizes, and some became pins that we could wear.

I still have our Creepy Crawler set in my attic and I also saved our Easy Bake Oven. This was another rainy day activity we loved. We spent all day baking little cakes. We quickly moved up to the double layer cake mix instead of the little packets it came with. My sister and I made little cakes for an eating contest. My brother and his friends always enjoyed participating in the eating of the cakes even if it took them away from their baseball or pickle games. Everyone was a winner, as all our little cakes disappeared quickly.

CHAPTER

1969 rolls around and two of my most prize possessions are my OUIJA Board and my Eight Ball. Both are birthday gifts from my parents. On those rainy days, I would love to make believe I could talk with spirit. Girlfriends would come over, and we would try to contact someone who was on the other side. (someone who was dead) Just as popular as garage bands, a good old séance in someone's basement was common.

One weekend we had a circle of girls in Kathy's basement. Kathy turned out the lights, and we all held hands and asked for a spirit to contact us. We all thought someone was trying to contact us; but, when one of the girls shivered and said she felt something touch her, we all freaked out. We were all screaming and running to turn the lights back on. After everyone calmed down, we decided to try to contact someone again. We got in our circle and held hands again. After a few more minutes of calling on spirit to come visit us, nothing happened; so we turned on the lights and moved on to another activity. I brought my Eight Ball, so we asked a couple of questions. Should we try another séance? "Reply hazy, try again." Should we clean our rooms? "It is decidedly so." Are we going to be millionaires? "Without a doubt."

Once when I was grounded, for a supposed inappropriate action, I asked my Eight Ball if I was going to be able to get ungrounded. It said "Yes." So I apologized to my mother and asked if I could go outside and play. She said "Yes". My eight ball was right! Ya, ya, I know what you're thinking!

On another day I started creating spells. I had a large sheet of glass that covered a dresser top. I discovered if you pour perfume on it and light it with a match, it made a beautiful blue flame. This made for a perfect "creating" ceremony. Although the blue flame was beautiful, I decided to do burnings with a candle and make it an outside activity. The thought of starting my bedroom on fire was unacceptable, and I dare not even think what would happen if my mother found out I had a flame in my room.

With a candle outside, I would write down on paper a certain outcome I would like to occur. Nothing bad, just positive things. Good grades, a new bike, no more lima beans, things like that. I would say a prayer for safety then fold the paper three times and say what I wrote three times. Then I would burn my paper. I believe creating thoughts for positive results in life is good. You don't need to do a burning to have a ceremony.

It was interesting, on many warm nights, you could find a lot of us on a friend's garage roof across the street. I wish I could remember what we were chanting. It was like another type of ceremonial gathering, everyone joined in the chanting. We would lay on our backs sometimes and just do some star gazing too. It was nice to share time with friends, looking at the beautiful sky.

On many summer days we were found roller skating in the

driveway, in and out of the garage listening to our record player. I put on "Sugar Sugar" by the Archies and "Spirit in the Sky" by Norman Greenbaum. I actually still have both in my collection of 45's. Of course I played Beatles tunes as well. What a fun, busy day; we would skate for hours just singing our hearts out to the great tunes.

We had a problem one day, when the arm of the record player started skipping across the records. I asked my father what we could do about it. He took our little record player to his workbench and quickly glued a ball bearing to the arm of the record player. It was the perfect weight, and it kept it from skipping across the records. Some of my friends had a penny glued to theirs.

As our crowd grew larger we changed up the games and took a break from the skating. We liked "Red Light, Green Light", but the most popular one was "Red Rover." This was a game that you could take out someone's arm if you ran into it hard enough. As we became professional Red Rover players, we learned to hold each other's arms at the elbows and not just hold hands. This would ensure a win, as nobody could break through our hold. "Red Rover, Red Rover, send Kathy right over!"

Another very popular summer evening activity was Hide and Seek at dusk, and into the night. There were twenty or more of us most times, so it was a lot of fun running all through each other's yards to find the perfect hiding spot, and then running to "ghoul" or the "safe spot" which was usually someone's porch, once you were found. Someone decided to change up the game a bit one evening and thought it would be fun to choose a partner. This became a boy-girl team thing. I remember I chose Karl, a boy from the other end of our street. He seemed to be a good person who could run fast and jump fences as well as I could. I had no desire to make it like a hide-and-kiss game as I suspect others may have wanted it to be.

Has everyone lost all common sense!? All of the sudden boys do not have cooties anymore!?

As another summer passes us by, we begin to look forward to new school supplies and school clothes. New clothes are great, but I am not fond of shopping and prefer to get in the store, pick out a few things, and get the heck out of there.

A lot of us were also thinking about Halloween. Our family would get a pumpkin, and dad would carve it with our help pulling out the seeds. Mom would rinse the pumpkin seeds and salt them to bake on a cookie sheet. It always smelled so good when they were cooking, and we always enjoyed the tasty snack. We had to decide what we were going to dress up as, this year. Most of us make our own costumes, but every so often you would see someone in a store bought costume. I remember making a poncho one year and wearing a sombrero that was laying around the house. When it's time to go "trick or treating," we grab our pillow cases and prepare to fill them several times. It's night time, but it looks like day time outside because every single porch light is on. The sidewalks are so crowded, you have to pass on the lawn. Parents claim they spend a hundred dollars on candy, and that was a lot of money back then.

We had a magical neighborhood I think. One of the dads at the end of our street put a pumpkin in his tree with a speaker in it. As you walk up to his house to yell "trick or treat," the pumpkin calls out your name, and says "Happy Halloween!" All my friends and I stop and just stare into the tree at the pumpkin.

We start yelling back to the darn thing in total amazement that it is having a conversation with us. We could stand there all night, but we must focus on the candy collecting goal. On to our next house, and after a couple of hours our mission is accomplished. After several stops back at our house for a candy dump, we have collected enough candy to feed us for years.

CHAPTER

Junior High School is an interesting place. The distance we had to walk was ridiculous, it's almost a mile away. (you know, uphill) John Page Junior High had a dress code for girls that said dresses or skirts are proper attire. Many of us thought it would be a good idea to get a petition to submit, to allow us to wear pants. Our legs were so cold in the winter, it made sense to change the dress code. We gathered enough signatures to change the dress code and could start wearing blue jeans to school. Yay! I don't remember much of Junior High school except for band class and one day when some girls decided to jam pack a toilet with toilet paper. The story goes, they tried to set the paper on fire, with success. The toilet then blew up. Boom

Junior high is a blur, so it's fun to look at the many photos my dad took. At the time, I didn't think I was a bank geek.

Lynn Britton

As the school year moves along, one of my favorite after-school activities is Girl Scouts. My mother was our troop leader and would tell me often that the daughter of the leader must be a good example to others and behave and stay out of trouble. "I never heard tell such a thing!" What if I don't want to be a good example!? Of course, I did behave, because I love and respect my mom. Our troop would meet once a week right after school in our school gym. Many of us started out in second grade as Brownie Girl Scouts and continued through the twelfth grade as Senior Girl Scouts. I remember when we were Brownies, we had to wait until we were the next level of Girl Scouts, Cadettes, before we could sell cookies. We were disappointed; but in the fourth grade we went door to door to our neighbor's homes to sell the cookies at only fifty cents a box.

It was interesting as we grew older, it became very uncool to be a Girl Scout, so we all decided to rename our troop. We were now "The French Club". If a fellow club member was curious during the day if you were attending the meeting this week, one would ask, "are you going to French Club?" Reply: but of course!

Karin, Lynn, Mom/Jan, Jeff
(Karin did a face plant on playground equipment.
Her face is not usually puffy. As an adult, she
is more graceful, dancing the Tango.)

We did some very fun and nice things. We made a lot of cards for senior citizens and took them to their living facilities. They were always happy to have us visit and talk with them for a while. At Christmas we would sing Christmas songs and were really quite good. A troop of thirty girls sounded very nice, and some of the residents joined in to sing with us too. A few years our troop went Christmas caroling through our neighborhood which was really awesome! We had our flashlights and song books and would walk down our neighborhood streets filling the night with beautiful music. After singing and receiving a lot of kind words from neighbors, we would have a Christmas party at someone's house and have hot chocolate and exchange gifts.

Our troop was really a very active one. We went camping at our near- by Girl Scout camp every year at least once. It's located up north a bit from our suburb, in Ortonville Michigan. They have many different units or sites to choose from and request for your troop to spend the weekend. Our troop was large and easily filled the big cabin they had. One large room was filled with many bunk beds, and another room was large enough for tables for all to be seated for meal time, along with a nice fireplace. There was also a large kitchen area with stove and sink and enough counter space and cupboards for all of our food. There were no bathrooms inside, so we had to go outside to the outhouses. We really didn't think much about it, this was camping. In the winter it was really cold so you learned to go fast. We would try to go to the outhouses before bed, so we wouldn't have to go in the dark and get out of our warm beds.

One evening, Suzanne and I had to go use the outhouse, and it was very dark outside. We both had our flashlights, so jammies, coats, mittens, hats, boots, and off we go. There were two separate potties so we each went in one. Due to the cold weather, we were hurrying so fast that Suzanne dropped her flashlight. Unfortunately, it took a bad bounce and went down the hole--yep in the potty mess. She yelled to me and said, "I dropped my flashlight!" I yelled back to her, "pick it up!" She said, "I can't" and "come look." We looked down in there, and the darn thing was shining away. We looked at each other with that shocked and "what the heck" expression, and just busted out laughing. As I held extra tight to my own flashlight, we went back to our cabin and told everyone. Now everyone wanted to go look at Suzanne's light shining in the potty mess. That darn thing stayed lit the whole weekend. So the highlights of our camping trip that weekend were sledding, singing together, cooking new meals and looking at a flashlight, shining in the potty.

Some years later, when we were in high school as Senior Girl Scouts, we decided we need to take a different kind of trip. We thought we should go visit New York. We had to come up with a fundraiser that would pay for a van big enough for all of us to ride in; Yes this was a road trip. Also, we would need a hotel for all to stay in and money for food.

We came up with the idea to sell geranium plants which turned out to be a huge hit. We walked up and down every street in our city going door-to-door. We would explain our plan for our Girl Scout troop to travel to New York. I think every house I went to bought a plant.

We rented a van and also had a car for luggage space. We hit the road and safely made it to New York. It is a very interesting place with many, many more people, some who think they should sleep in doorways. It is nothing like our little city in Michigan.

We have plans to go to the Statue of Liberty for one of our

days. That was a crazy climb up the longest spiral staircase and then back down another set of spiral stairs. It took a long time as there were people on the stairs, both sides all the way from top to bottom. I really enjoyed looking out the openings in the crown of the Statue of Liberty. When we asked if we could go up into the torch for a better view, we were told by the officials, it was not safe and the arm could fall off; we all said "ok". Not going to argue that one.

We traveled on the subway a few times too; that was an adventure. There were only about twelve to fifteen of us total. Girls and adults. So you would think it would be no trouble to stay together and not get separated. The subway train cars stop, doors open, you get in and do the head count. Well, one time not everyone was in the subway car, talk about panic. Fortunately there were trains running quite frequently, and we all remembered what stop we were getting off. Everyone was safe, and then we decided we better make a plan for separation issues in the future. We never did get separated again. Phew!

Back in Michigan

Another one of our activities was roller skating at the roller rink. What a blast! We would go as a Troop or on our own. Some of us took lessons--I think mostly to earn a Girl Scout badge. Oh what fun to learn how to do "shoot the duck". I wouldn't dare try anything so dangerous now, at my cautious age of sixty. Well, I will try it, but not with wheels hooked on my feet. I think I could handle the ever popular Hokey Pokey still.

We would happily make a huge circle, put your right foot in and put your right foot out, put your right foot in and shake it all about! Do the Hokey Pokey and turn yourself around, that's what it's all about! I like the memories of the song and how happy we all were with the simplicity of the whole dance as we sang and clapped along all together. It is one of my happy songs.

Having a happy song is wonderful. I often hum a tune; it just makes me feel good. I think everyone should try to have at least one happy song, I have a few. "Twist and Shout" always reminds me of happy times and groovy dancing. When The Beatles sang "I Want to Hold Your Hand" on The Ed Sullivan Show, in 1964 that made a lot of people happy. Our family watched on our black and white television. (with no remote)

Some songs or jingles sometimes get stuck in my head. Not really realizing, I keep singing or humming the same thing over and over. Often, it irritates someone else and they end up telling me, "stop it"! Ugh. Then we both start laughing, and that makes us happy.

CHAPTER

High school years were exciting to me. I decided to continue with my percussion interest. Most of us started taking band in the fourth grade, so we were getting pretty darn good. Many of my classmates could play so beautifully. I just loved listening to the perfection when our band was playing. What a wonderful way to start the day.

We had so much talent in our concert band; several went on to make music their career. We did the usual amount of concerts and enjoyed it very much. Our concert band was also the marching band so we enjoyed doing the halftime shows at the football games each Friday. Our marching band practiced an hour before school started to make sure we had enough practice for our show music and formations. Seven in the morning is early to be starting band practice, so my parents were very happy when I got my driver's license. It became more exciting around Homecoming time as we decided to enter a float into the parade to represent the band.

We organized float parties at someone's house and sat around for hours and hours making Kleenex tissue flowers and drinking Towne Club pop. We would fold the tissue, tie it with string, and then fluff it into a beautiful flower. It was a wonderful social activity. I swear, I alone, made a trillion flowers.

Later in the school year, many of our concert band members attended the Solo and Ensemble Festival. Seven of us, in the percussion section, decided to perform as a septet together. The Solo and Ensemble Festival was held at another school facility, so we had to pack up all our equipment, bass drum, snare drums, cymbals, etc., and find a parent with a station wagon to get our instruments to where we were going. We practiced quite a bit to our advantage. We were awesome, and the judges thought so too, we received a "1" for our score! That's first place--the best. We all received a blue medal, suitable for pinning on our band jackets.

During the school year, I also took a class to learn how to write papers. This was for college preparation, so I would not have difficulties while in college English classes.

I remember writing a ten-page paper on witches and all their hardships, and how they were accused of ridiculous crimes. I decided to take the side of the witch who was inappropriately accused of wrongdoing. So many women were killed due to fear and stupidity. Some were drowned, and I also wrote, how they would kill alleged witches by burning them at the "steak". My teacher made the ever-popular comment in the margin. "Was it T-bone". Don't you just love a teacher with a sense of humor? I do! And I got an "A".

Another class in high school was driver's education. That was an easy one. Everyone was attentive because we all wanted to drive. After passing the book-work portion of the program, we were to begin what they called "road work". It's kinda funny how you learn what not to do while sitting in the back seat of the car while your classmate almost kills you because she hits the gas instead of the brake! We survived, and probably gave the teacher some extra gray hairs, but we are now legal drivers. Look out, here comes the class of 1974, the largest graduating class from Lamphere High School, and we are ready to hit the road. Gremlins and Dusters and Pintos, oh my!

Yes, we are now behind the wheel of some of the most cool cars ever made. Just check out the Woodward Dream Cruise on the third Saturday in August each year. The cars are still around and more beautiful than ever.

In 1972 I was given the driving privilege of the 1964 Pontiac Catalina. Yay! The powder blue boat car! When you tap on the button on the floor to turn on the bright lights, a green light in the shape of Chief Pontiac's head, lights up. Very cool. It also has those little triangle windows where you can open them up and direct the breeze. It looks cool when you rest your left arm on the open window and hold on to the frame of the triangle. The windshield wipers also went out, then in, not left to right together. Whoever changed that didn't live where it snows.

A girlfriend and I would go out for an evening of cruising on one dollar of gas. We each chipped in fifty cents and were good for the night and also got us to early morning marching band practice.

One evening Debbie was able to get her parent's car for our girls night out. It was a woody! You know, the station wagon with the wood paneling on the sides. We loved it! So we gassed her up and were on our way. This was an interesting vehicle as it was only able to have two accessories running at a time. So when it became dark, we could have the headlights on and the radio. If it started to rain, the radio was turned off so Debbie could use the windshield wipers. Those were the good ol' days!

We could pile a lot of us in the good old woody too. We liked the flat space in the rear of the vehicle. No seat belt law in Michigan until 1985.

If Debbie had to roll the back window down due to steamy windows, there was a lovely fragrance of car exhaust.

One weekend we decided to organize a newspaper drive for a band fund-raiser. We had some people picking up papers and meeting at the high school while some people would dump the newspapers at our school for us. One of the guys had a pick-up truck that we filled to the tippy top of the flatbed to drive to the recycle place. To keep the papers from blowing away as we drove them to the recycle place, a few of us had to lay on top of the newspapers. I still remember lying face up going down 13 Mile Road and looking up at the I 75 bridge as we drove under it. It was crazy!

As soon as my parents read this, especially my dad, he is going to tell me "you're grounded!" I hated being grounded when I was younger, it seemed like it was an overused punishment, frequently. I swear the oldest gets the blame for everything! Oh well, once again I survived. It is really funny these days, to hear my dad say, "You're grounded!"

On a winter morning, it was time to go to school, and I was getting into the Catalina. I put the key in the ignition and she did not want to start. So I did what any teenage girl would do. I hopped out and opened the large powder blue, boat car hood and sized up the situation. I had to go back into the house for my special carburetor tool. I decided the little flap door thingy wasn't functioning properly, so I wedged the spatula in the little space where air must enter. I walked back around and got back into the car. I turned the key and she started up! The spatula was now a permanent tool that I kept in the car. I look at these new car engines these days, and they look like a glob of plastic. If something goes wrong I just say a prayer.

When I was a Senior in high school, my sister started her first year in high school. We had three grades in high school in those days. Tenth, eleventh and twelfth. So now my sister becomes a licensed driver too, and I have to share the Catalina with her. I am not pleased with this at all. It's a good thing I had already cleared it with my parents to decorate and paint the powder blue boat car for celebration of my graduation from high school.

Karin and I made it work, but we both had different activities; and, after my graduation from high school, I decided to shop around for my own car. I considered a car loan from a credit union and was a bit excited. I'm not sure why going into debt is exciting, but becoming independent with responsibilities feels good. I had been working ever since my mother hired me to iron pillowcases and my father's handkerchiefs. She used to sprinkle water on the handkerchiefs and pillowcases with a pop bottle-and-cork sprinkle attachment in the bottle. Then she would roll each of them up and place them in a large plastic bag. I made two cents for each handkerchief and five cents for a pillowcase.

After working a fast food position, I worked as a cashier at The Abby Theatre's". This job was flexible with my college class schedule. I saved up some cash and my parents took me used car shopping. I ended up with a 1969 Chevelle, it was a great little car. I put a new cassette player in it with new speakers, and played Beatles tunes louder than anyone I know. While I was cruising around town enjoying the fine sounds on my new stereo system, my sister was in custody of the Catalina. Since Karin decided to become a cheerleader in high school, we had different social circles. Can you believe she loaded up the beautiful powder blue boat car with cheerleaders and drove it up Lamphere Hill? What were these girls thinking? This is inappropriate! This is no small little pile of dirt! It's a very popular sledding hill behind our high school. Guess who else is going to be grounded when dad reads this!

In 1893 at the World's Fair, in Chicago.
Pabst Beer was given the Blue Ribbon.
(Learn "something new", fun fact)

CHAPTER

After graduating from high school, I went to college for almost four years. I decided that I didn't really want to be a school teacher and took a different path and went into restaurant management. I met my first husband as he came to the company I was working for as a Manager Trainee. I was the Manager in charge of training new personnel for the company so we spent a good amount of time together. We began to date and enjoyed each other's company. After dating for about a year, we decided to move in together and get married. We had a nice little apartment--thank goodness it was a two-bedroom. We learned we had our first daughter on the way. Rachiel was born in August of 1983. I was so happy and thought how good life was and how God Blessed us with a beautiful baby girl. I enjoyed being a mom, and, when I would pace the floor holding Rachiel in my arms, I would pass a mirror and say, "look how good we look together". This was true love.

Then in November of 1984, we were blessed with our second daughter Danielle. I remember when I was pregnant with Danielle I had doubts about having enough love for another child. I could not figure where more love would come from. So I asked my mother. I told her I love Rachiel so much, so how do you make more love for a second baby? Mom said, "you just do". Of course she was right, and as soon as Danielle arrived, I loved her so much too. I had so much love for each of my daughters and thanked God for yet another miracle. There is no end to the love available. When April 1986 came along, God blessed us again, and our son Jonathan was born. I had no doubt about enough love for him too.

I was so happy and so very busy. Three children to love and receive love from. I love all the first moments and everything in between. Everything is such a miracle. The first word, the first tooth, and playing peek-a-boo. I am grateful to God every day for my beautiful children.

I took all three kids to the grocery store one day just for a quick trip; we only needed a few things. Jon was in the seat part and the girls were riding in the big part of the shopping buggy. As we headed up to the checkout, we passed a lovely display of cheese and crackers. This display was designed like an artificial Christmas tree and had five tiers of large square bowl-like shelves. Each tier had one million of those little packages with the four crackers and cheese in them. As we passed the lovely top-heavy display, Rachiel decided to grab a package. To this day I have never, ever seen so many little packages of cheese and crackers slide so far across a floor, it was like the darn things had little matchbox car wheels attached to them. It was kinda funny, but at the time I thought I should pick them up as quickly as possible and be on my way. My lesson learned here was not to get upset over little things like spilled crackers.

I was going to be the stay-at-home mom and raise our children, and my husband would be the income provider. Unfortunately that plan did not work. After four and a half years of marriage I filed for divorce. I find myself a single parent with three small children, and am looking for work.

I applied for a paraprofessional position with the Head Start program in our school district. There were about twenty of us that applied for one position. After a week of interviews and waiting, I received a call informing me that the job was mine. I was very happy as it was a perfect part-time position. I also started doing office cleaning jobs in the evenings where I could bring the kids. I needed to make money, not spend it on daycare and babysitters.

I was very fortunate to have a very supportive family. My parents helped in every way they possibly could. My father purchased shrubs for my little house, and we planted them together. My mother would come over on Halloween and pass out candy so I could take the kids trick-or-treating. My sister was living in Cincinnati and would knit the kids blankets for their beds. My brother would fill in taking the kids to activities like dad/daughter, Girl Scout pumpkin-carving night. They are truly wonderful people, and there are many more times I am so grateful for them.

Each night as I tucked my children into their beds, I would kiss them goodnight and repeat my mantra to each of them. "I love you infinity, infinity times, don't let the bedbugs bite or the moths." I would also say a prayer for our safety and good health and include my whole family. It is a long list, but that's ok.

The next morning, after working my shift at the school, I came home and had the afternoon for cleaning the house and doing laundry. I recall watching the TV show "Little House on the Prairie" as I folded laundry.

One episode had the father taking many jobs just to pay the bill at the mercantile. (The general store) He was taking on the jobs that nobody else wanted to do. He got so dirty and smelly that the nasty child in the show started making fun of him to his daughter Laura. When Laura talked to her father about it. He told Laura, you should never be ashamed of any job you do as long as you do your best. He had the most positive outlook on many life situations. He wore the most awesome boots too; his boot straps would hang down the sides, so he could pull them on at the beginning of each day. I related his boot straps to strength.

I thought to myself many times, I am a positive person, so now I have strong boot straps. When it gets tough, I will grab my boot straps and pull up hard and keep going.

Honestly, I did not see another option, so each morning I would thank God for another day and pull my boots on. I would say, "ok boot straps, start walking!" It is kinda corny, but it put a happy tune in my head. Single parenting became very difficult at times, and I could see how some may want to throw in the towel. There was no way I would do that, I love my children and am going to do my best to provide for them. There were many times when I was unable to make a full utility bill payment, so I became the queen of payment plans.

As another school year begins, it brings a bit of stress. The school requires you to purchase all kinds of supplies, as well as needing new backpacks and new clothes. Also, school pictures that cost way too much, lunch money, field trip money, and don't forget to donate a box of tissues.

A few months into our new school year, I received a phone

call from Jon's teacher, he is in Kindergarten. She told me we need to have a meeting asap, and the principal will be joining us. I said, "I can come this afternoon." When I checked in at the school office, the teacher met me, and escorted me to a little closet room with a table and a few chairs. As our meeting began, the teacher told me she believes my son has ADHD. She gave me a few examples of his behavior, which I believe are normal for little boys. She then suggested I put him on Ritalin.

My anger and protective mother instincts kicked in. I do not understand why a teacher is diagnosing my son, so I looked her straight in the eyes and told her, my son is a normal little boy and I do not think he has ADHD.

I calmly said to her, "there is no way you are going to drug my son." I got up from my chair and said, "good day." I walked quickly down the hall to get to the door. As I was about to leave, the principal called to me. I turned, and as she came closer to me, she said, "I agree with you."

What is going on here!? I had no response for her, I didn't want to be rude. I cannot believe what just happened! I am wondering how many other parents have been called into their crazy meeting room, and how many more little boys lives are being altered unnecessarily. Later in the week I decided to ask other teachers why there is a push to put kids on Ritalin. Nobody wanted to talk about it.

As we enter the two-wheeler phase of bikes, I don't recall Rachiel having too many issues with removing the training wheels. After a few practice runs, she was ready, and off she went. Danielle was a little different story. When I ran along side of her, she was good, but every time I let go of the bike, she would head straight for the street. It was necessary to run my fanny off to catch up to her. Balance was no problem; steering needed work.

It was very interesting with my son, Jon. He must have been watching Danielle and decided she was wasting time, doing it wrong. He hopped on the smaller two-wheeler we had and just took off. It was wonderful, no running to save another life, phew.

My father decided to take the kids ice skating one weekend. We have open skating in our local ice arena, where the girls are taking some lessons. My father purchased a small pair of hockey skates for Jon, so as the girls skated around the ice, the guys put their skates on. When they stepped onto the ice, Jon fell once, got up and went like the wind and never fell again. I decided to put him in skating lessons too. I thought he was too young, but he is handling it just fine. During one of his lessons, a gentleman asked me if I had thought about putting him in hockey. I didn't know anything about hockey and just wanted a little something for my kids to do on the weekend. I learned very quickly how expensive hockey is and how very time-consuming it is as well.

While the years go by, Jon becomes an excellent player; I found myself the Manager of two of his teams. Danielle was interested in hockey too; and after the men in our little hockey association agreed to let a girl play on the boys' teams, she also became an excellent player. I soon found myself the Registrar of our Youth Hockey Association, a Board position. Many of the moms of the hockey players applauded my courage to try to straighten out the mess that was obviously ongoing with this association. That only lasted two years; I gave it up as both Danielle and Jon were drafted onto travel teams. Jon played on the Junior Vipers one year, which was very fun. They played out of the Palace in Auburn Hills which was very nice. I will never forget the day I was watching Danielle's practice, when she played for a Honey Baked Travel team. There were Scouts watching too, and the Scout from Yale came over to ask me about Danielle and her college preference. Danielle said she did not want to move so far from home. So that was that.

Meanwhile Rachiel decided she likes softball. They did not have enough managers/coaches, so unless they found someone, these seventeen girls would not be able to play. Yep, you guessed it. I found myself in charge of a girls softball team, with the local Softball Club. I did that for twelve years as both my daughters played second grade through twelfth grade. One year I coached two different teams because Rachiel moved up and they needed coaches! And just to top it off, I became a Board member and the Fundraiser Coordinator. It's funny, I remember being so busy changing diapers and thinking it will ease up when they can go potty by themselves, reach the light switches and buckle themselves in. A minor miscalculation on my part.

The girls also attended dance classes. They both were awesome little tappers and jazz dancers. I made a point to steer clear of any volunteering with that organization. Too pooped to participate.

After school one afternoon, my darlings and I headed up to our Meijer's for a few food items. We also needed to go to the shoe repair place they had conveniently located in the store. As we stood waiting for our turn at the shoe repair place the kids were busy touching everything in their reach. As I tried to keep them out of trouble, I decided I better take off my sunglasses. As I was removing them from my face, one of my darlings needed to be pulled back over closer to me. Somehow while grabbing at kids, the stem of my sunglasses went up my right nostril, far enough to make my eyes water. Finally the gal behind the counter asks how she can help me and also asks if I am ok. I said I am fine and gave her the shoes to be repaired. I didn't really want to tell her I just stuck my glasses up my nose. Ugh!

Moving along, we are now ready to go shopping. Oh goody, they have little miniature shopping buggies for kids to push around in the store. At first you think it's really a cute idea; but, when you have to keep an eye on three little darlings who now think Meijer's is a race track, you wonder who thought this was a good idea. It must have been a man, right! Not only do you have to make sure they aren't crashing into anything or anyone, but the kids think they need to fill up their buggy with cookies. We shop swiftly, letting each one choose a couple of items for their buggy. Now the food shopping portion of our program is completed. All four of us head up to checkout, it was kinda cute, each of us pushing a buggy. Just when I thought we were safe, a store employee asks the kids if they would each like a free goldfish. I'm saying "no thank you," and the kids are whining about how much they need a fish. So each of them now has a baggie with a fish added to their buggy. We check out and head for the door, another fine day at the grocery comes to a close. When we get home, the kids each put their fish in the fishbowl. We already have a fishbowl and fish food from the last free gold fish from Meijer's, which only lived for one day. I will pencil-in fish funerals on the calendar.

As far as our school studies were going, the kids were doing well. Everyone can read and write, add and subtract. When we moved into our home here, it was thirty years ago. I started placing artwork and homework in neat little piles to keep for future admiring. As the piles grew bigger and bigger, I decided to open up the attic door and keep all my treasures there. I recently came across a little one-page paper assignment by Danielle. It also has my signature on it, so it was one of those that the teacher found inappropriate and sent home for a parent signature, and we had to return it to school. This was a scare tactic that I was immune to by now. We all make mistakes, that's how we learn. My son had a teacher in third grade who did not care for boys in her class. I wish I would have saved all the little stupid notes she sent home. "Jon talked in class", "Jon wanted a drink of water", "Jon wanted to go to the bathroom". When did normal become annoying?

I decided that Danielle's paper was suitable for framing.

The word Faggot is
Used as a disparaging
term for a gay or homo-
sexual man.
    Sometimes Faggot and
lesbian get confused.
Lesbian means A gay or
homosexual woman.
    I dont think it's nice
to call a gay person a
faggot, just like it's not
nice to call an overweight
person a lard ass.
    A person who is a faggot
can do the same stuff
a regular person can
do.

                By: Danielle
                    Karnes

                    Lynn D. Karnes

CHAPTER

After working with the Head Start program for eight years I decided to give it up as well as my office cleaning jobs. My children were a bit older now and could walk home from school together and get themselves into the house safely. That way I could take a full-time job instead of many part- time ones.

In 1998 I started working for a popular hardware store chain. This was not one of the large chains, just a local one here in Michigan. I recall we had seventeen stores. I worked at the Corporate office, in charge of the salvage/return department. I had my own office which was located in-between the warehouse and the front offices. I was very happy with the pleasant and intelligent people I now worked with. Previous jobs seemed to be a collection of unhappy souls. Yes, the school district personnel, not all, but many.

My work schedule was Monday through Friday, but they also offered extra hours in the warehouse on Saturdays. It was just a half-day, so we could send the truck drivers out to the stores with more product they needed for the weekend. I decided to check it out and put in a few extra hours. As I was working, one of the delivery truck drivers, who also filled in sometimes on

Saturdays, came over and introduced himself. He said "Hi I'm Jay" and told me he is the Manager of Shipping and Receiving at one of our stores. We had a nice little chat and then both had to get back to work.

Later in the week a girlfriend and I decided to go check out a little bar in Royal Oak that had karaoke. I wasn't sure about the karaoke thing, but it turned out to be pretty cool. As a guy was singing an old style jazz-ish song, I found myself tapping my feet along with the song. We were sitting at the bar, so our backs were turned away from the stage where people were singing karaoke. As we ordered and got ourselves settled in, the song ended. The crowd went crazy clapping and cheering! The very popular singing artist came over to say hello. It was Jay, the Shipping/Receiving Manager from work.

He joined us for a beer and conversation. We talked for a little while, and he asked me if I would like to hear a specific song. I always liked an oldie called "Secret Agent Man" and asked him if he knew it. He said he did, and I thought he sang it perfect. It was getting late, so my girlfriend and I prepared to leave to go home. As we were leaving, Jay asked if I would like to go see a movie sometime. I said "sure".

I had been dating a little, but nothing serious. A dinner here, and a drink there. So I figured why not have a movie thrown in too. Jay and I set a date to go out. We found out, we really didn't have a movie that we wanted to see, so we decided to skip the movie thing and went to the karaoke bar. I always enjoyed an evening of singing and dancing, we met a lot of nice people. Some could sing very well and some were not good--we applauded equally for all.

One evening my kids were getting showers and preparing for bedtime. After shower time, we had a little snack and then brushed teeth. As always, I would tuck each one in and tell them "night, night, love you infinity, infinity times." "Don't let the bedbugs bite or the moths." Now all my babes are safe in their beds. I decided to watch a little television--a popular show, Ally McBeal. This show is hilarious! As I am watching the show, something made me think about how I would like to date just one person. I didn't know who I should pick so I asked God. I said, "Dear God, please give me a sign to show me which guy is Mr. Right." After the commercial, when the show returned, all of the sudden the song "Secret Agent Man" was playing as part of the show. I said out loud, "Oh my God!" "That's incredible, what a really good sign; can it be that easy?!" So after a year of dating Jay, he got down on one knee, with diamond ring in hand, in my kitchen, and asked me to be his wife. We were married on Dream Cruise day, in our backyard August 19, 2000, surrounded by family and friends at the best party ever, and we haven't been to a movie yet.

WEDDING PICTURES

Danielle, Rachiel, Lynn, Jay, Jon
And Arthur is first to congratulate us!

It is May of 2002, some friends at work decided to go to a psychic for entertainment. Jay and I decided to do the same. We thought it's something new and different and we hope it will be fun. It was a thirty-minute reading and was very interesting. Ms. M. used tarot cards. She placed the deck of tarot cards in front of me and asked me to cut the deck and asked my birthday. I said March 11, she says "you're pretty psychic yourself, and how long have you been a workaholic" and said "you better take a vacation," as she flips one card after another. She told me, I am a farmer with a green thumb, connected to mother earth. Also, that I know about alternative remedies and holistic health. Then she mentioned my second career will be natural healing. Phew, what a lot of information in a short time, good thing I recorded this. Ms. M. told me not to worry about failure, "we all fail, it's a part of life." Next, she said if I ever need to sue someone in court, even if I am 104 years old, I will win.

Good to know! After twenty minutes Ms. M. asked if I had any questions for her. I did, one was about my children. She turned over another card and said "it says here you are supposed to have three children." "How many do you have?" I said "three" and smiled. She had mentioned earlier that I was intuitive and asked if I was doing any psychic work yet. I said "I just picked out a deck of tarot cards." She had a big smile on her face and said with a laugh, "you are going to love it!" She also mentioned that I knew a lot about vitamins. Ms. M. said my three children were also intuitive. I later learned through my studies all three of my children are Indigo Children. That explains a lot of things!

I am happy I didn't let the school district drug my son, or convince me Danielle's paper was a problem.

My oldest sees spirit and the other two have incredible

premonition dreams along with all three being sensitive to the good and bad vibes I guess you would call it. I recall when Jon was middle school age, he woke up and told me he just had the worst dream ever. It was about a fire in a home in Berkley on 11 mile road. That same day we saw the news, there was a huge fire on 11 mile road in a house. Thank goodness nobody was hurt.

I asked Ms. M. if she knew about any past lives of mine. She asked me if I had the desire to move down south, and if I was from the south. She said, "I think you were a hillbilly, and I don't mean that in a bad way." We lived off the land and were very natural. "It was happy happy times." There was a bit of a pause and she said, "except," then another pause, "you know how protective you are of your children?" "In that lifetime you lost your kids to some disease or something of that time." "In this lifetime you are afraid of losing your kids, and it comes from the past life when you lost your children." "That explains your overprotectiveness a little bit." I have never forgotten what she said next. She said, "let me tell you in your deep mind that you will never lose your children in this lifetime."

I think that explains my workaholic nature. When I was single parenting, I would do any job to keep my children. I had a fear if I could not provide for them, they would be taken away from me.

Around this time, the ulcer on my right cornea decided to flare up. This virus first showed up when I was eighteen years old. I hadn't had any issues with it recently but now in 2002, it's back. (Almost 30 years) It is very painful and requires staying out of the light, I must wear sunglasses even if it isn't sunny. After weeks and sometimes months, the flare up would end, leaving scar tissue on my cornea, which caused some loss of sight. To control the virus, I had two eye-drop prescriptions. During an eye appointment, my doctor suggested to me that a cornea transplant might be a good idea. My instincts tell me this is not a good idea so I told my doctor I needed time to think about a surgery. I discussed my concern about surgery with my family and some friends. A girlfriend I met through work gave me a phone number of a chiropractor doctor who also does alternative healing. I made an appointment and it was amazing. I had to invest in a lot of vitamins/supplements, and had to take about seventeen a day, I recall. Dr. B. told me, regular doctors don't cure you, they just usually cut things out. He also said "we will kill this virus; there is no need to have surgery." I was very relieved.

That started my quest for more knowledge about vitamins and minerals. I first researched all the supplements I was taking to cure the virus on my cornea. It is incredible! Natural food seems to have an endless supply of healing for our bodies. I started experimenting with all different kinds of tea, mostly to boost the immune system.

I invested in a lot of books on herbal medicines, natural healing, crystals, past lives, dream interpretation, Angels (my favorite) and many more. I started acquiring so many I had to buy a book shelf unit!

I started reading many books, I was impressing myself. This is many more books than high school and college put together. I finally found subjects I am interested in. I started growing a lot of my own vegetables, berries and herbs. It is absolutely wonderful to go outside and pick a handful of fresh strawberries or raspberries for an early morning breakfast.

Lynn Green

I became interested in the body, mind, spirit festivals that were around the area. They were fascinating, so many wonderful metaphysical things going on. Of course the very popular psychic readers were there. They had titles like, Spiritual reader/Medium/Clairvoyant or Psychic Medium or Channel - Intuitive Counsel and Energetic Healing. With approximately thirty different readers to choose from, how do you know which one to pick?

Well I went for the one with the chocolates on her table for a treat. Very nice choice, and I received a lovely reading. I asked about crystals being used for healing. Miss J. said yes, you will use crystals when you do your energy work.

Just as my book collection grew, I found myself with all kinds of beautiful crystals. From Amethyst to Rose quartz to Lemurian seed crystal and more.

CHAPTER

It is now the year 2003.

Rachiel has decided to move out and into an apartment with her boyfriend. I am not thrilled with her choice, but she is nineteen and there is no room for discussion on her part. I thought this would be a mistake, but I decided to support her decision and help her move her things. I even gave her some extra furniture we acquired when my grandmother passed away.

After a few months, Jay and I found out our first grandchild was on her way. This was exciting to me--now we get to plan a baby shower and welcome a new baby. We planned the baby shower for a weekend in July, nothing very big, just a few friends and family.

On June 25th I was at work and received a call from Rachiel. She was at her scheduled appointment for an ultrasound to make sure all baby things were a-ok. Rachiel was crying on the phone and said the ultrasound showed something wrong. They had her in an examining room, but would not give her any information. I left work right away and went to the hospital. The hospital decided to admit her so they could monitor her and baby. The fluid around the baby was basically nonexistent so after a very rough night, no sleep, and Rachiel threatening to rip bed rails off, they decided to finally give her some pain medication and induce labor. Raven was born on June 26th. Mom and baby are doing very well.

The next weekend, Raven was the star of the show and came to her own baby shower. There was no need for silly games; we pretty much spent the time holding Raven as Rachiel opened the gifts.

It was almost a year since they moved into their apartment, when things changed. Rachiel and Raven were moving out, and we welcomed them into our home. It's been quite a few years since we had a crib set up. Now there are six of us in our little house (not on the prairie).

One Saturday morning when Raven was about a year old, Rachiel had to go to work. That left Raven and me a whole day of play. After our busy morning, Raven picked out a book for us to read before naptime. We usually sat on my bed for story time, so we fluffed up the pillows to lean against and started reading the story. We both must have been very tired and fell asleep before the story was done. The next thing I knew there was an Angel waking me up, it was like a voice in my head. The Angel was next to my bed from floor to ceiling, pure white, and translucent. As I looked at the Angel I said "hi," and rolled over and tried to go back to sleep. The Angel touched my shoulder and guided me to look at Raven. She was hanging off the side of my bed, her little feet dangling towards the floor. Her little shoulders and arms were still on my bed, the Angel was next to her. I quickly sat up, scooped Raven up, hugged her, and gave her a kiss. I got out of my bed, holding Raven and took her to her crib. When I turned around the Angel was not visible anymore but I thanked the Angel for keeping Raven safe. I don't like to even think what could have happened if she fell off between the bed and wall. Thank you, Angels!

As 2005 rolls around I find myself working full time and helping raise my granddaughter. Raven is wonderful and such fun to be around. I remember watching her at her little table and chairs, coloring and drawing. I came home from work one evening, Raven was standing next to her little table, looking out our front living room window. In her right hand she had a pencil and was drawing something. She was not looking at the paper, but looking towards the window. She moved the pencil back and forth making a little picture. When she was done, I walked over to praise her. It was on two pieces of paper that were overlapping each other. When I looked at it, it was an Angel. I thought I had another Indigo Child in the family. I studied a bit more about Indigo and Crystal Children and asked a few psychic friends about Raven being a Crystal child.

It was interesting, Raven and I went to purchase some fun things at a shop we had not been to yet, in Royal Oak. We were greeted by the owner and her friend who was a psychic. We introduced ourselves and started looking around at all the goodies. The psychic said to me, you are a high healer and Raven is a crystal child. I thanked her and explained I was curious, and that at first I thought she was an Indigo. We found some candles and crystals I liked and Raven found some polished stones she liked as well. We thought this was a great place to find fun stuff, and told them we would be back.

Since my children were all pretty athletic, I liked to take Raven outside and play a lot. We would play with the little hockey sticks, draw large pictures on the driveway with colored chalk and ride her little bike. Raven had a bit of an issue with skinning her knees. She would be running along and wham, she would be on the ground. Sometimes she would skin her knees when they were already skinned. Geez we went through a lot of bandages. Oh no, now I have that band aid song stuck in my head. "I am stuck on....... cause........stuck on me." Ha, so I had a thought, if we set up one of those little plastic sandboxes we might save her little knees. Raven loved it, and began creating all kinds of little cakes, pies and cookies. She used my measuring cups to pretend to bake with. Isn't it funny how all your cooking utensils and pans soon become outside play toys?! I decided to ask my husband if he would build us a bigger sandbox in our back yard. "No problem-o" he said. We now have an eight foot by ten foot sandbox, and we are loving it. We set up an area next to the sandbox complete with table and umbrella for Raven's cooking experiments and they continue to this day.

As time is scooting right along here, my daughter Danielle has blessed us with our first grandson Christian in April of 2006 and a granddaughter in November of 2007. Danielle was trying to think of girl names but nothing seemed to be clicking. So, where does one look for the perfect girl's name? We went to my bookshelf and found the Book of Goddesses. We looked through the book and came to the name Kali. Danielle liked it and made it so. Kali is also a Crystal child.

Life happens, and their biological father decides to move along. So my little house, not on the prairie, but is getting scary, is home to two more grand babies, I love it. My house organization goes out the window, as the living room is now a bedroom and toy room. We now have eight of us in our little house. Talk about a plethora of fun and love under one little roof. I am grateful for my little house and beautiful family.

CHAPTER

In 2007 my job at the hardware store chain came to an end. Due to the very bad business decisions by the administration/ owners, the business went belly up. They filed for bankruptcy, and everyone started looking for new jobs.

I applied for a teacher position at an after-school program through our school district and was hired on the spot. This is curious and thought provoking, back into the same school district I go. It was a part-time position so my daughters could work during the day, and I would watch the grand babies.

They would come home, and I would head out to my job.

My Program was held in the gym at an elementary school where we could set up tables for snacks and homework at one end of the gym and have sports activities at the other end of the gym. Floor hockey was a very popular indoor sport, both boys and girls enjoyed playing. While the hockey got started, we would clean off the snack crumbs and get out craft projects. I had many talented and creative students kindergarten through fifth grade. Some days I would set out a craft project and find myself needing more items like glitter, glue and yarn so they could keep creating away.

Some of the younger children liked taking paper, pictures and markers and setting up a fort under the tables. Then the signs, "girls only" or "boys only" would be taped to the entrance of their fort. I thought it was cute. Did I mention, I am a professional fort builder? Forts are cool.

I started to create some weird and fun activities. I noticed the children liked to throw or kick the footballs up into the rafters. I went to the dollar store and bought two plungers and also some very long pieces of rope. I took the rubber part of the plunger off the stick handle and asked my husband to drill a hole through the rubber part where the stick was. I then put the rope through the hole and tied a square knot. I learned how to tie knots in Girl Scouts--see it is cool to be a Girl Scout! I have invented the plungrr game. (Pronounced-plung grr) I gave one of the plungrr games to a fourth grader, to test it out for me. The object is to throw it high enough to go over the ceiling beams, while holding on to the other end of the rope and then reel it back. All the children stopped what they were doing and watched as Brad, prepared to throw the plungrr up. Ready, one, two, three, he threw it way up there, but it was just shy of going over the beam. The odd shape is a bit of a challenge. Now everyone was yelling "I want to try it!" So we made our first rule, you get three throws per turn. Brad was ready and looked very determined to make sure he made it over the beams this time. He whipped that thing so hard it easily made it, and you would have thought he won a world series game. The kids cheered so loud and ran over to form a line for a turn. It's a good thing I made two of the plungrr game, it was a wonderful activity that all could enjoy. The kids started making up new games as they attached a hula hoop to the plungrr once it was over the beam. They would throw the football through the hula hoop as one of the games, swinging the hoop slower and then faster for more of a challenge. This plungrr game turned out to be a bigger success than I imagined. The creative games that came out of these wonderful children was really rewarding to watch.

One of my other favorite activities was the toilet paper contest. We had those huge rolls of toilet paper and the kids just loved wrapping each other up in it. Some would create the ever-popular mummy or wedding bride. We had several children get all dressed up in the t.p., and then they held a fashion show. When everyone decided they were done dressing up with the t.p., I would get my leaf blower out. I had each child gather t.p. and bring it over to the middle of the gym. I turned on the leaf blower, and they would put their t.p. in the air stream which I aimed at the rafters. Whoosh, whoosh, whoosh, over and over again the place looked like a blizzard. They could do this for hours, but after forty five minutes, I gave notice for one more time and then we need to clean up. It's interesting how they all liked to use the brooms and dustpans in the school.

I am truly enjoying this job, I like playing hockey, coloring and showing kids how to make paper airplanes. Once I showed the kids how to make the planes and they took it from there. We were having best-decorated plane contests as well as throwing them for distance contests. The kids played with them inside and outside. They would throw them off the top of the slide and then through the steps of the slide. They were always thinking of new and improved games.

As I continue with my day to day activities, I start to notice my knees are hurting a bit, especially when I am bending down to help do clean-up time. I don't know who said "it's your knees that go first", but this thought pops into my head. My shoulders, hands and wrists are in pain as well, which I relate to getting older and take some ibuprofen. My eyesight is also changing, so I purchased a little pair of those reader glasses; wow, what a wonderful invention these are! Its great to be able to read the small print, which doesn't seem small to others. One challenge is remembering where I sat them down when I took them off. I started grabbing an extra pair at the store until I ended up with five pair.

I guess you just need to put one in every room and then one in the car.

The year 2011 rolls around, and life is busy as can be. I am meeting my daughters new boyfriends, and my son has a wonderful girlfriend too. My grand-babies are energetic beyond belief. I remember my kids being energetic but it seems I'm running a little slower and low on steam. It's funny when it finally hits you, we really do get older.

As I am getting ready to finish up another day at the school program, many of the children are getting picked up by their parents. One of the moms is crying and is very sad. I asked her if there was anything I could do to help.

She said no, that her best friend Mitzi just passed. Mitzi was a little doggie that I had the privilege to meet several times. Such a cute little thing, and you could tell she thought she was so tough. Mom would hold Mitzi in her arms when we were outside on the playground. Mitzi would see a squirrel and have the fiercest growl. It was quite humorous really. Little dogs that think they are big dogs are funny.

The pain of her loss was evident as she told me she believed that "our animals are a cruel joke being played on us." The emotions from the loss of a pet are overwhelming; they are family. We love them so much, they have the most beautiful unconditional love.

We had the darn cutest little kitty. When Raven and I would be reading a book upstairs on my bed, Fluffy would come rip-roaring up the stairs as fast as she could. Then running across the room she would fly up onto my bed and skid across. She would stop, look at us, start panting like a dog and then take off back down the stairs. We would laugh and laugh at Fluffy. She would do this several times until she exhausted her little self.

On occasion she would add a little fart along with the panting; again we would laugh and laugh. Fluffy was a stray that we found and took into our home. Unfortunately, she only lived to be about three years old. She had such a fun personality.

We also had a black lab, we named him Arthur. We met Arthur through a friend, I knew from a previous job who was giving away free puppies. We fell in love immediately. Arthur, like Mitzi, is a fur buddy-full of unconditional love.

It's a Monday morning, March 28, 2011. When Arthur did not come upstairs and put his two front paws on my bed to wake me up, my heart sank. This was his routine every morning for sixteen years, Instead he was laying in the kitchen on one of his favorite rugs. It's 6:30am; I am preparing to go to work, running the before-school program at the elementary school.

Arthur did not want to eat either, which was very unusual.

I gave him several servings of water. He has Horners Syndrome which required my assistance when eating and drinking. I had to leave, it's 6:40am. I told Arthur I would be right back and pet him before leaving. It takes me approximately ten minutes to get to work. The morning program is only one hour long.

All the way to work I prayed for Arthur, I asked God to let him live until I got home so he would not die alone. I asked Angels to go to Arthur and to wrap their wings around him.

When I was at work, I checked my watch and it said 7:10am. I looked at the clock on the school wall and it said 7:44am. Something interesting is going on with time. My watch was still running, as I noticed the second hand still moving around the numbers. I tried to reset my watch, I never had any trouble before, but today it was impossible to reset.

I could not get the little knob to pull out so I dismissed it. I believe time was slowed, so I could get home to Arthur.

I left work quickly, my car clock said 8:01am. When I got home, Arthur was laying on the landing by the back door where it was very cold. I picked him up and carried him to his bed. He was so very warm. I thanked the Angels for loving him and keeping my baby warm. I laid Arthur on his bed, holding his head in my right hand and petting his neck and back with my left. I looked into his eyes, he looked into mine.

I said "Arthur, I love you so much." "It's ok, you can go." He took a breath and let it out. He then passed away in my arms as he lay in his bed.

I thought it was 8:15am. and I covered Arthur up. I started making the call to the vet for cremation arrangements. It took a while through the tears flowing, the woman was so kind and said "take your time."

Thank God for grandkids. Christian and Kali came with

me to take Arthur to the vet's office. Grandkids will keep you so busy; they kept me from crying the whole way there. I can honestly say I have never cried so hard in my life. I hurt real physical hurt as well as emotional. When I tried to talk, I broke down in tears. I kept saying to myself, get a grip! But it is really hard! I have a headache from crying, I actually thanked God for aspirin.

The day continues, and I am now on my way to the after-school program at the elementary school. I am remembering how Arthur did bed checks on all our family members every night and woke me up each morning. I miss him opening the bathroom door and entering whenever I was in there. I will only have to make two eggs, not four in the morning. We loved our fried egg breakfasts. At one point I thought we were going to have to get a chicken.

It is now late Monday night, 11:30pm. I am totally exhausted and going to bed. As I take off my watch, I notice it has stopped and It says 8:20.

I believe Arthur has corrected me on the time of his passing. Love is such a strong energy! My dog reminds me!

I am grateful for my family, my friends, the vet people and the Angels. All the kind words of love through cards, emails, text messages, hugs and warm wings. I am grateful for God's Love.

No matter where or when you are, you are always loved.

Thank You God for blessing my family and me with Arthur. He gave us unconditional love every day for sixteen years.

I still wear my watch, and have not put a new battery in it. It is my reminder of Arthur and his love.

CHAPTER

10

As April of 2011 gets here, Danielle and her boyfriend Chris are getting ready to close on a house and move in. They have been looking at a lot of houses and finally found one they both like. I can't believe how big it is.

My question is, who's going to clean this thing?

It is a beautiful home, and I am sure they will fill it with love.

After all the moving of everyone's stuff into their new home, they are just about set. All the dressers and closets have been filled, new bedspreads are on the beds, and cute boy rugs are in Christian's room and pretty princess rugs in Kali's new bedroom. Now they are doggie-shopping, of course. They decide on a labradoodle. They could have just bought a small horse; they are about the same size, good grief. My question is, who's gonna clean-up the yard?

2012 turned into a very eventful year. Both Danielle and Chris are working full time; and when school ended for the kids, summer vacation started and so did my gramma duty. I was off work from the school district for the summer so Danielle would drop the kids off in the morning for a fun day at gramma's.

We had a lot of fun riding our bikes up to the parks and school playgrounds. We did some craft projects and went through at least a hundred containers of Play Doh. I purchased a bunch of really big buckets for some outside water play time. That was a huge hit, especially when I bought twenty bottles of dish soap. Chris was in charge of picking the kids up after work on his way home. One evening when Chris came for the kids, he was acting a bit different--he seemed a bit nervous. We were chatting a little, and Chris slipped in a question to me. At first I misunderstood what he was asking due to his quiet voice. After a minute of discussion, he wasn't getting the response from me, he anticipated. So he spoke up a bit louder and asked me for my daughter's hand in marriage. Wow, that was very cool, you don't hear about good old American traditions like that anymore. I was impressed, and said yes, of course.

Chris proposed to Danielle on June 8th and they decided to get married on August 18th. Yes, of this year, so everyone goes into stress mode. Danielle asked my husband, Jay to walk her down the aisle. My daughter Rachiel is the maid of honor, and my son and his girlfriend Heather, and of course Christian, Kali and Raven are all in the wedding. Holy moly, we are all running around like crazy people.

After several trips to the clothing stores, everyone has their proper attire, except Jay's pants are like peddle pusher's. That's what we used to call them in the 1960's. You know, flood pants. We had a really good laugh at how ridiculous his pants looked and then jumped in the car for a quick trip back to the tux shop for an exchange. Phew, all good, and we are ready to go. I had my new dress and new uncomfortable shoes and was ready too. The wedding shower was great, and the wedding rehearsal and dinner went very well. Now it's time to hit the hay, It's wedding eve.

I woke up the next morning at six o'clock, not feeling very well at all. I went downstairs and looked into the bathroom mirror. My bottom lip is very puffed up and the lower portion of my face is swollen. I freaked out a bit, put a lot of ice on my face and decided to get dressed. I am taking myself to the emergency room at Beaumont Hospital. I get there, they put me on a gurney, and the nurse started to walk away. I spoke up and told her I have a bit of a situation here. I said "I am the mother of the bride, and I am supposed to be at my daughter's house at noon for photos."

All of the sudden my bed is speeding down the hall; I'm hoping we don't crash into something. The nurses and the doctor were fabulous, so nice and very kind. They pumped four drugs into me through an IV so my face would get back to normal size. After about two hours, they sent me on my way with three prescriptions. Although my face was back to normal, I am experiencing fatigue, and can barely stay awake. I should have asked for a puppy upper.

At Danielle's house, the photographer was busy getting all the pre-wedding shots. All the sudden one of the bride's maids had a dress tear along the zipper. Major wardrobe malfunction! Two of the other bride's maids were out the door, on their way to pick up a new dress, after calling the dress shop and telling them to have it ready at the door. Mission accomplished, we are now on our way to the wedding. We arrive a bit later than planned, but it's a beautiful day. It's an outside wedding and friends and family are gathering on the lawn around the parking lot. It's so nice to see all the out of state folks. As we are greeting guests and hugging relatives I have my own wardrobe malfunction. Has anyone had their control top hose roll down? For heaven's sake.

The wedding was so beautiful, Chris and Danielle look fabulous as well as the entire wedding party. Everyone is so happy, what a wonderful wedding. Chris is a U.S. Marine, so he was in his dress uniform. Some of his Marine buddies in uniforms also took part in the ceremony, swords and all. It was all very impressive to me, and I was honored to have a Marine escort me to my seat.

CHAPTER

11

It is now September of 2012 and everyone is getting back into the rut of life. Back to school time! I was happy for the grandkids to get back into their routines, and they were happy with all their new school supplies and new clothes.

I felt I needed a bit of a break as I was still feeling very fatigued and now started to have noticeable breathing issues. I found myself waking up in the middle of the night gasping for air. I took some over-the-counter medications for stuffiness thinking I may be having allergy problems. That wasn't working very well, as I tried many different remedies. It was becoming hard to inhale and I found myself trying to take deep breathes just to get a little air. My whole body was beginning to feel as though it was going to fail me. My joints were so painful, my knees, shoulders, elbows, wrists, fingers, hips, ankles and toes. Migraines were occurring as I became a lot more sensitive to light. I was literally in pain from head to toe. I made a doctor appointment to find out what in the world was going on.

As I prepare to retire for the day, I decided to prop up my pillows to help with my breathing. Unfortunately, that wasn't helping, and I awoke when I stopped breathing. I could usually relax and calm myself and slowly inhale, but this night was different. I was not able to inhale and became very scared. I tried to relax and calm myself, but I was still unable to breath in. I tried and tried to inhale and could not. I began to panic! I got out of bed and tried to walk but collapsed to my knees. I realized I had drawn my last breath and started to mentally prepare to die.

I began to pray. I remember telling God, I want to stay; and, if you let me live, I will never drink beer again.

The next thing I know it's morning and I'm in my bed. I know I had assistance getting there. I am so grateful; I keep thanking God and my Angels over and over.

I decide I better get myself ready for my doctor appointment so I can find out what is wrong with me. A thought comes to mind, "for the love of crackers!, why did I say I will never drink beer again!?" I wonder if I can ask God for a do-over? Could I change that to lima beans, please.

My doctor appointment was interesting. There were many tests, breathing and blood, x-rays, etc. She diagnosed me with C.O.P.D. and gave me two prescriptions for inhalers. She also referred me to Dr. C., a Rheumatologist. I had no idea what a Rheumatologist's specialty was, but there was a six-month wait for an appointment. I could not believe I had to wait six months to find out why my body was experiencing such pain and fatigue. I scheduled the first appointment available, which fell on my birthday in March of 2013, how the heck does that happen? I also started a search for an earlier appointment with any Rheumatologist and found one with a three-month wait. I booked an appointment to get blood work done at Dr. M's office.

In January of 2013, I was diagnosed with Lupus. I only had

a couple of appointments with Dr. M. and decided to go to my March appointment with Dr. C. I liked all the information from Dr. C. and the professional people in her office, so I asked Dr. M. to send all my test results to my new Doctor. I started reading everything I could about Lupus, I had no idea what it was. I had my pity party, thinking my life was over and wondering how long I had to live before my immune system which was attacking my good cells in my body, was going to take me out. At this point I began to wonder how much of my breathing issues were really C.O.P.D., or if perhaps it was a Lupus flare-up attacking my lungs. I also thought about the cornea transplant issue. My instincts not to have the eye surgery were right on. My immune system could have attacked a new cornea.

One week after my Rheumatologist appointment, I had to go back to my primary care doctor for a terrible pain in my right hip. That was on a Monday. She did an x-ray and checked me out and found nothing wrong so I happily left and went home. On Friday I found a couple of spots on my lower back; it looked like a small rash just above my right hip. I didn't think much about it, and I went to bed. When I woke up the next morning I had such an awful pain again around my right side, hip area and was covered with this rash. I asked Raven to check out rashes online, and we compared mine to some of the pictures that were posted. I called my doctor and told her I think I have shingles. She asked me to describe the rash and immediately called in a prescription for shingles.

I also researched natural remedies for shingles. I found a couple of things and decided, what the heck, I am going to try them. The shingles rash is very painful, you don't want to touch it, you don't want to bend or bump into anything, and sitting down is a whole new experience of painful movement. I think I controlled it pretty well, but a month of shooting pain along with my lupus discomfort was off the chart of ridiculousness. I could use a beer! Lol, just some humor for God.

Instead of feeling sorry for myself, I decided to get myself together and start doing some positive thinking and positive manifesting. I had to remind myself, I am a Healer. I am a Reiki Master, and I do energy healing with God's love. I decided to polish up my Reiki skills and concentrate on becoming a healthy person.

I grabbed my boot straps and said "start walking."

As May 2014 approaches, we are anxiously awaiting the arrival of our fourth grandchild. He is due to arrive at the end of the month. Christian and Kali are ready to be the big brother and sister and good helper to mom and dad. We shall see how that works.

I received a call from Danielle around two in the morning on the twenty seventh. She said "it's time!" I got in my car to go pick up Christian and Kali, and bring them to my house. Of course nobody could go back to sleep, so we talked about the new baby brother and what he will look like and be like. Kali was very concerned about his health and what he would look like. I explained that some babies are born with special needs, some have no arms, and we love them so much no matter what. She was listening very intently, and I added that I was sure her new baby brother would be perfect.

We all agreed to get a little rest. That afternoon the kids were excited they were skipping school and very excited to meet their new brother. Raven was happy to miss school as well and go with us to meet her new cousin. So off we go to the hospital to meet Sebastian. On the way to the hospital, we are still going over babies, and ten fingers and ten toes. When we got to the hospital room, we met Sebastian, oh my gosh, what a cutie! He is tightly wrapped in his little receiving blanket. After everyone was done hugging and kissing each other, Kali walked over to her mother, and asked her, "does he have both arms?" Danielle just looks at me, like "what the what?!" At this moment, I wish I had the super power of invisibility. Danielle assured Kali he did have two arms and showed them to her. I had to explain our late-night discussion. Sheesh, I'm glad we all had a good laugh; kids say the darndest things. I will make sure my grandma wisdom and expert discussions are not misleading in the future. Good grief.

On August 11, 2014, I pulled into my driveway and into my backyard when the weather decided we need to have more than an average rain. I looked up at the gutter on my garage due to the noise it was making. The rain was coming down uncommonly, ridiculously hard and fast. It was so crazy the water was pouring over the rims of the gutters. I got out of my car and ran into the house as quick as possible. My normal routine is to let our doggie outside but decided he could use his piddle pad inside, for fear he may float away as the rainwater was collecting into a lake in our yard. I went downstairs and pulled my laundry from the dryer and went back upstairs. I opened up my front door and was in a bit of shock; my street had become a deep river flowing rapidly to the east.

All the sudden I heard a thumping noise coming from the basement, it sounded like a boat motor. I ran down the stairs and saw water shooting up from our floor drain and noticed the water was gathering around my fan on the floor. The fan was shooting water out the back like a boat motor. I quickly ran to the plug and unplugged it. I then grabbed the plunger and placed it over the floor drain to stop the water from coming in. I had to stand on it. As I did that I heard something pop and I heard water again. I had to get off the plunger to go look around the wall. There was the drain cap from the main cleanout floating across the floor as water was gushing in from there too. I freaked out and ran over and grabbed the cap. I was desperately trying to put the cap over the hole it came from; but, with the power of the water coming in, I could not get the cap in place. I kept trying over and over again with no luck. I couldn't even see where the cap was supposed to screw back on. As I began to cry, I said, "Dear God, I need help." Something covered my right hand very gently, from wrist to finger tips. I looked down at my hand and we were putting that cap in place and very quickly screwed it on tight. The water stopped coming in from there.

I jumped up and began running around pulling plugs out of sockets, but decided since the water was above my ankles that I better get back upstairs. The water was still coming in very quickly from the floor drain. I quickly grabbed the bleach bottle, ran up the stairs and basically took a bleach bath at the kitchen sink. I just took a washcloth and scrubbed myself with the bleach.

As I stood at the top of my basement stairs, watching the water rise higher and higher, I saw Raven's little doctor kit float by. I said, "well there's something you don't see every day." We ended up with about one foot of water and sewage in our basement, which was just over the first step.

The next few days were spent taking everything out to the curb for fear of contamination. Thank goodness, my son Jon came over to drag basement furniture out to the curb. I figured we lost about ten thousand dollars' worth of property. That figure didn't include the new washer and dryer and furnace repairs. Washers and dryers were in high demand in this area due to the fact that they don't work after being submerged in sewage so it took a while to get new machines. It took weeks before a furnace person could get to us too; everyone needed a furnace guy. We finally had someone out and gave us the good news that we did not need a new furnace--we just needed a new circuit board. Of course we had to wait; circuit boards are in high demand as well. We survived by candle heat for a few evenings; and, at the end of September we were blessed with a working furnace.

After the flood, I thanked God. It could have been much worse as many neighbors had more than a foot of sewage enter their basements. This was a horrific ordeal, not just for the loss of property, but the health concerns were huge. The smell of our neighborhood was putrid as everyone was placing the entire contents of their basements at the curb for garbage pickup. Unfortunately, it sat for weeks as the cities worked to get it all picked up. So many people lost so much; it really made me realize how things can change in an instant.

CHAPTER

12

I have lived in my house now for thirty years and decide since my basement is all cleared out, I should clean out my attic.

I find myself with an attic full of kid memorabilia, and I am ready to dig in. My children are now ages thirty, thirty one and thirty two. I really have been putting the task off, due to the amount I have accumulated. Once I started though I could not stop. I pulled my little stool into my attic area, had a seat, and started looking at each piece of paper and each artwork project. "What wonderful artwork I have here!" You know, the hand print wreath--also a glitter-and-glue noodles masterpiece. I also found a rice-and-aquarium-stones project with enough glue used to keep them on the construction paper for eternity. I love the cotton-ball snowmen and the oatmeal-container pilgrim person. I think I can use the pilgrim person for a Halloween decoration. It's kinda scary. I am pulling another pile of papers towards me, and tossing a few of the kids' homework assignments in the recycle bin. I lift up a triangle-shaped artwork item. It is on green construction paper and a manila folder for strength to hold the weight of the lovely green-and-red, beautifully-placed lima beans! Oh, my gosh! I love this so much! One of my children made lima bean artwork!

It's fun to see all the kind words teachers wrote on all the assignments. I found a lot of full sheets of paper with spelling words on them that we were supposed to cut out and make into flash cards. Oops, oh well.

LIMA BEAN ARTWORK PICTURE

Approximately fifteen years ago, we rescued another little kitty that was hanging around in our backyard. Jakey is a beautiful and very friendly little cat. She does not like to come in the house, so we made her a heated home inside our garage. As well as feeding her daily meals, I give her a special good-morning treat. One fine October, Monday morning, (2016) I was stepping out my backdoor to give her the treat just like always. This morning our welcome mat started to slip away from the house under my right foot. As I began to fall down, I tried to lean back and catch myself with my right arm and hand to stop the fall. In the process my left leg, at the knee, bent back and to the left. The pain that shot up my leg told me, legs aren't supposed to bend that way. As my bottom hits the threshold the screen door slams on my left knee. I really didn't see that coming!

Now I am jammed in the doorway and must free myself. With a few choice words, I throw the screen door open and roll out of my house onto the driveway. (graceful Lynn) I get up and limp over to Jakey; she is probably thinking I have totally lost it. It's amazing how a cat can sit so calmly and watch an accident unfold. I open my left hand to give her the Colby cheese I had cut into little tiny bites for her. I chuckle to myself, thinking about the "help I've fallen" necklaces. It's interesting how I never used to think about getting hurt while doing everyday activities or riding down "suicide hill". Even a dog toy on the floor poses a threat! Thank goodness there are no Barbie doll high heels hanging around.

My life has been blessed with many different jobs and activities. It has always been interesting, challenging and always a learning experience. Many of my friends and family have had one main job or career plan for their life and are very successful. Others have had several different jobs and are also very successful. Some have made teaching a career, and the medical field is also a popular one. Some are hair stylists or seamstresses which I think are wonderful talents. One of my classmates was blessed with his career of drawing and painting very large and beautiful whales.

I believe I am to successfully acquire and learn as many different tasks as possible which has led to meeting so very many people. I've had good jobs and bad, from Program Director of school programs and teaching Preschool, to Department Head at a hardware store headquarters and shipping and receiving at many different companies. I am a daughter, sister, mother, wife, grandmother and aunt. I am Lynn, and I am enjoying life.

The very best and most challenging position I think is parent. I am so proud of my three children and their kind and considerate nature. My daughters have become wonderful mothers, and I am so very blessed with grandchildren from them. At bedtime I hear them tucking in my grandchildren, and the mantra continues on. They have added to it and tailored it to their own specifications, but the main message is there.

Love you infinity, infinity times.

Both Rachiel and Danielle have decided to permanently tattoo the infinity symbol on their leg just above the ankle. Danielle schedules important events on a date with an 8 in it. (8 is an upright infinity symbol) Her wedding was on 8-18 and Chris even made sure he proposed on the 8th of June. It's interesting how that "love you infinity" stone I threw hit the water and is rippling out.

With all my learning lessons, I am grateful to see Divine Intervention. These are magical moments for me--miracles! I am grateful for every day I draw breath and can take a walk or play.

I am grateful for my parents who put up with me, especially in the 1970's. My sister and I kinda, really put them through hell. I believe I could write a really fun and interesting book about our adventures in the 1970's.

With my diagnosis of Lupus, I believe God has sent me the message to slow down, and sit down! It's my turn to accept. I am happy to receive this healing time and am working on my purpose in life.

As life continues, I often wonder what I am supposed to be learning from my so called, life lessons. I think it has a lot to do with the choices I make; I do feel older and wiser. I have enjoyed writing this book very much, and have learned I should have studied a bit more on punctuation and sentence structure.

My Question is,

So what if..... the Hokey Pokey really is what it's all about? Happy song!

May God, Bless You.

Printed in the United States
By Bookmasters